Respect the Code!
Laws for
Career Strategies
& Codeswitching

Respect the Code!
Laws for
Career Strategies &
Codeswitching

Mo Davis

IMPRINT/Mo Davis

Copyright ©2018 by Mo Davis

All rights reserved. No part of this book may be reproduced or transmitted in any form or by any means, electronic or mechanical, including photocopying, recording, or by any information storage and retrieval system, without permission in writing from the author.

Published by Mo Davis

Cover Designed by Rob W.

Printed in the United States of America

ISBN 978-0-692-04971-6

Acknowledgement

To my Heavenly Father, who placed this book on my heart. "Obedience is better than sacrifice" was all that I was reminded of constantly, so Thank You Father.

Dedication

I dedicate this book to My Family:

My husband who I love to the deepest level, who patiently allowed me hours upon hours to hide off into my secret spot in the house away from the kids and get this book written. My handsome and amazing son who brings me joy every time we chat. He is my number one fan and future business manager. My daughter Zoe, her spunk and constant desire to mimic me drove me to want to do better and be a strong example to her. My Grandmother Dorothy Singleton who taught me forgiveness & true love. My beautiful Mom, De Rogers for overcoming so many obstacles the world threw at her and giving me the first example of a strong woman.

To My Clients:

My career counseling clients that allowed me to go deeper to the root of their obstacles and in turn minister to myself as well.

To My Muses Anita, Keisha, & Domonique

And my amazing book writing coach E Danielle Butler --Thank you

FOREWORD

I am truly honored to be asked to write the Foreword for this powerful book, *Respect the Code! Laws for Career Strategies & Codeswitching*. In my 25+ years of codeswitching as a person of color between the professional world, family life, time with friends, etc., this is the first book that specifically lays out the importance of codeswitching, especially for persons of color.

It also provides strategies on how to implement it successfully in the workplace. While you may say that I've heard this term for years, what can this book do for me?

Well, in a day in time, where anyone can basically find out anything about you at any moment, it is important that we have a healthy balance on how to RESPECT THE CODE and know when to successfully code switch so we can have not only career success but true success in all areas of our life.

Additionally, I commend Mo Davis for sharing her story in this book. Her ability to open up the pages of her life and provide details on how she was able to overcome many obstacles will be the 'seed' that someone needs in order to turn their life around and reach new heights in their career and personal life.

However, there is a key point that I don't want you to miss from the story of Mo Davis. She chronicles how the valuable lessons of codeswitching started at a very early age. That is when she realized the 'epiphany' in her life or as the saying goes, 'she became WOKE,' and recognized how she could receive extraordinary outcomes in her life through codeswitching.

I truly believe that by reading this book, you will be on a path of success that will many times SHOCK YOU because you are now in a new stratosphere of possibilities.

Read this book, take notes, reflect, but most importantly take action! Never forget to RESPECT THE CODE!

Chance W. Lewis, Ph.D.
Carol Grotnes Belk Distinguished Professor of Urban Education
Director, The Urban Education Collaborative
University of North Carolina at Charlotte
Web: http://www.chancewlewis.com

Introduction	10
Self-Identity	13
Defining Success	15
My Turning Point	19
Monique or Becky: A Lesson in Voice Altering	20
Who Me? (Receiving Criticism)	23
Appearance & Presentation	28
Video Vixen Body, Oprah Winfrey Mind	32
Interview: Research & Proposals	37
Get & Maintain the Job	43
Work Esteem and Self-Motivation	43
Competing against myself not you	46
Resting !@$#% Face	47
Tone and Communication	50
Office Norms	54
Relationships	57
Kissed alot of frogs but not that one	57
Inappropriate Communication	58
The Case of the Ex	60
Keep Your Friends Close & Co-Workers Closer	63
Entrepreneurship & Small Business	69
Career Assessment	69
Small business still a business	71
Laws in Effect	73
Resources for Personal Development & Career Transitioning	76
LINKEDIN TIPS	78

MOCK INTERVIEW	80
Index	83
Respect the Code Dictionary	85

Introduction

I'm really glad you took the time to read this book. This is more than a book to me, it is a guide to career success. In many ways, I believe my life journey prepared me to write this book. Life lessons, various job titles, work environments, promotions and layoffs, all purposed to help not just me but also you! While reading this book, you will understand how to be strategic in your career and be empowered while also code switching.

I wear a lot of hats (wife, mom, career strategist and more), and I love empowering others. In my coaching and strategizing, I noticed something, I am not the same in every environment. The way I am with my family is not the same way I am with my manager. The way I am with my manager is not the same way I am with my colleagues. The way I am with my colleagues isn't the same way I am with my friends. The way I am with my Southside friends is not the same as I am with my Northside friends. This can go on and on. But I'm making a point here. In order to be successful you must recognize your environment and be able to Respect the Code, aka code switch! The dictionary's definition of Code switching references mixing languages and speech patterns during a conversation. It usually happens when a person speaks multiple languages.

However, this generation has made code switching even broader than that. If you are at work writing a proper email with proper grammar and all accurate punctuation but you suddenly get a text from a childhood friend and instantly grammar and spelling are out the door, that's also what code switching is.

Just think about it, do you go in a library turned up, loud, and obnoxious? Do you attend a funeral wearing a bathing suit, high fiving everyone and throwing a beach ball? Absolutely not, because you RESPECT THE CODE!

I know that I may have some readers who say, "Code switching? That means you're being fake. I just like to keep it real". Or this is my favorite, "They either love me for me or leave me be. I'm not switching up for anyone!" Well, this book is especially for you! Why? Because, you *have* to do some code switching in your lifetime, especially if you have a diverse circle. On the other hand, if your desire is to be successful but your circle of friends isn't diverse then you may need to consider broadening your horizons as well.

I researched different people and their code switching habits. One person that displays the most sophisticated form of code switching is former President Barack Obama. Now before I share the various instances, I'm aware that some folks either really love him or really hate him but all things considered, most respect him. He graduated from a prestigious school, married a beautiful, successful woman, is an awesome father to their children, held two terms in the presidential office, and never attached to ANY scandal that could defame his name or family.

Now that we've addressed that, I monitored him with regards to code switching and here's what I observed: Obama was definitely known for switching it up. One video in particular shows him in the basketball locker room with NBA players and coaches. He gave firm, traditional handshakes to the white coaches and players but when he made it to Kevin Durant, he "dapped" him up. And then went back to handshakes with the other players.

His willingness and desire to adapt made a statement that said, "I'm not too stuffy to be cool, but I'm not too cool to recognize that everyone doesn't receive the same greeting." President Obama can also be witnessed switching up his vernacular, mannerisms, even linguistics (in one instance by speaking Spanish at a predominately Hispanic rally) at the right times.

Let's take a quick pause and reflect on your life and different instances where you should have code switched but you didn't. What was the outcome? How would you react if the situation presented itself again?

If you're like me, you may have cringed at the thought of your erred ways. I wrote this book so that we can move from those awkward encounters to one where you operate in the confidence of code switching in your life, family, and career. I will share some of my less than stellar performances. I will also offer some suggestions on how you can avoid some of the obstacles I faced. Within this book, there will be an opportunity for you to continue reflecting and readjust your course for career success.

We will candidly address self-identity and the impact it has on our career choices and success. We'll look at the role that appearance and presentation play on the career journey. We'll also tackle the job hunting process and strategies for maintaining optimal success once you have landed your role. Ultimately, this book is about you. It is my hope that you will find tools here to help you succeed whether you are just entering the workforce, changing opportunities or building your own empire. I want you to believe that you can do anything you set your mind to do.

Are you ready to Respect The Code and move towards your success??? Let's go!

This book comes straight from my heart to you! No hidden agenda; no lead in for the next book. Simply put, this book was written to help you become the man or woman that you are meant to be in life. This book will appeal to all genders and races of individuals although it is written from a person of color's perspective. This is for the person that desires to encounter success but may have obstacles or issues that got in your way. Not success from another person's definition or the world's view, but your appointed and ordained success aligned with the will of God!

Self-Identity

I've always struggled with my identity. In the course of my life I've been an actress, acting coach, talent rep, technical college instructor, leasing & marketing professional, Executive Assistant, Recruiter, and a Workforce Program Coordinator, just to name a few. I wanted so badly to do it all but I learned quickly that if you ever want to make God laugh, just tell Him YOUR plans for your life.

Thinking back on my career choices, I excelled in each position, even to the point of being offered management level promotions. Soon after that promotion conversation would take place, I would run and change jobs or careers. You see I wasn't afraid of failing. Just the opposite, I was afraid of my success. In hindsight, I believe that is why I enjoyed consulting so much, because I didn't have to marry one job. Oh yes I know what you're thinking, "She probably had the same mentality with men!". And you would be absolutely right! Before my husband, and of course before I knew who I was, I ran. I have been engaged multiple times! Each cancellation or "indefinite postponement" was initiated by yours truly. It was an identity problem that I just didn't want to face. But I digress...

At that time in my life, professionally I was afraid of my success. You see, I believed if I became a manager and gave it a true "Yes" I'd have to stick with it and sacrifice my other dreams. At the time my aspirations to be an entrepreneur placed me in a different mindset that didn't include only corporate success. At one point, I stopped and asked myself, what was I good at and what was I passionate about? What was I DESIGNED to do?

Take some time and reflect: Is what you're good at also what you're passionate about?

_____

_____

_____

One thing that was consistent in every career was my desire to speak positive affirmations into various individuals and help them achieve goals shared with me, no matter how big or small. I think about when I had my baby. The doctor was nowhere around except to make sure nothing went wrong. But my midwife, wow! She encouraged me, motivated me with her positive affirmations and made sure I was positioned properly to deliver. That's what I constantly wish to do in every part of my personal and professional life: support and coach men and women on how to give birth to their dreams. I thrive on giving suggestions on routes to take, strategies to utilize, as well as tools and resources needed along the way.

I discovered who I am career wise through prayer, experience and a career assessment. (We will talk about career assessments further in this book.) Just note that faith without works is dead. You can be talented, smart, and quick witted but without proper training and works (effort) there is a limit on how far you can go. Think about Lebron James, he is one of the best but if he didn't practice hard, research his competitors, sacrifice eating healthy versus junk food, and have a winning mindset, how far do you think he could have gone?

I discovered who I am spiritually and personally through tons of disappointments, childhood abuse, good times, and bad times. Finding out what makes you tick, what you are afraid of, and your patience level are all connected to your why. Why am I an executive assistant instead of an executive? Why am I a fast food cook instead of a chef? Neither position is more important than the other, because you have to start somewhere. However, learning who you are, will give you a better career map to where you are designed to go.

Before we go any further, I'd like to take some time to reflect. What do you do as a career? What do you aspire to do? Why?

_____

_____

_____

_____

_____

_____

_____

_____

_____

_____

_____

_____

_____

_____

Defining Success

Growing up on the southside of Atlanta, GA my family and I lived in a two-bedroom apartment off of Godby Road. And by the way, one bedroom was my mom's room and the other I shared with my sister, brothers and my baby cousins when they lived with us. I enjoyed watching strong, beautiful women on TV and connecting to them in my head. In reality, I didn't see a lot of "beautiful" women in positions of power. In my hood, the "successful" women were broken down in three categories:

    1. Dope Boy Girlfriend/Wifey

    2. Exotic Dancers

    3. Beauticians

I used the term beautiful as a relative term. At one time in my life, I believed beauty to only be aesthetically attractive and I soon figured out that was one sided and wrong. At the time, my definition of successful was whoever appeared to have a lot of money. From the three categories above, right away there is one I never ever attempted to pursue. Which one do you think that is?

If you said 3. Beautician, you are absolutely correct! Ha! Yes, out of those three choices as a young person, I considered everything but doing hair. I hated doing hair; I simply was never good at it.

However, dope boys were another story. There was something about me that attracted them. Maybe it was the brokenness of not having a father around, I felt I needed someone that could take care of me. I was just a teenager when my boyfriend would take me shopping, pay my pager bill, and pay small bills at my moms. My mindset at that time was, "Hey as long as I'm not doing anything wrong, using their money for good should keep me in the clear!" And "What I don't see, I don't know" but even I knew at that time, I was lying to myself.

As far as the exotic dancing, I was too frightened to dance in the nude BUT an alternative in Boston was go-go dancing. Go-go dancing meant dancing in a club environment to techno (or whatever music the club was known for) with really short shorts on and a top. I Go-Go danced during my college years in Boston, MA. I would go to school on the weekdays and go-go dance for extra cash at night and on weekends. I remember actually feeling proud of myself that I made so much money in one night and I didn't have to take off "all" my clothes. That was what I thought success was at 19, making a large sum of money. Needless to say, I had a very distorted view on success.

I met my first serious boyfriend at the nightclub where I worked. His name was "E", and he was a Jewish guy from Boston. He taught me so much in the art of codeswitching. He never ever stopped being who he was at his core. But he respected the code of every environment he encountered. His family was from a town called Newton in Massachusetts. They were pretty established and did well for themselves. With me, he was the most patient person, but at the club he was direct and to the point. When he was around his mom and Bubbie (grandma) he switched it up and was the respectful son. He had dealings with certain types of individuals that were "bosses", and he maneuvered through their world untouched but still respected. E taught me how to code switch in various environments. Basically, it's not just about what you say in code switching, but it's what you don't say as well. Sometimes it's what your body language is saying.

Being around true Bostonians I always thought that they spoke differently. After a while I could feel my slow country slang being sharpened like their speech patterns. I spoke quicker and for the most part took "umm" out of my vernacular. He introduced me to so many social categories of people, and I learned by watching him. I discovered I had great interpersonal skills, a knack for discerning people, and great business acumen.

Yes at 19 years old my idea of success was changing and go-go dancing felt beneath me! One day, E simply said, "Hey I don't want you to work there, you're better than that." I said ok and that was that! My short stint as a go-go dancer came to an abrupt end. It's almost like I needed some direction to get me out of there. I wanted someone to tell me that I was better than that, to reassure me.

Fast forward to today, prayer and counsel revealed to me that this was a form of rejection that I carried with me a huge portion of my life. It's sad but I thought I needed validation and reassurance that I was smart or special.

After making a decision that I knew was for the best, I prepared myself for the journey I had ahead.

I previously mentioned taking a career assessment to help me discover who I am. I hired a career consultant to counsel me on my career. In the counseling, I realized that I was on the right track but my idea of success was inaccurately connected to money. I discovered that true success is connected to understanding why you do what you do for a living.

Reflection: What's your definition of success? Do you believe that you are successful? Why? or Why not?

_____
_____
_____
_____
_____
_____
_____
_____
_____

My Turning Point

If there was ever a beginning point where the rubber meets the road...making a decision to stop go-go dancing was it! I didn't quite know what I wanted to do but I knew that I wanted to make enough money to not "feel" poor, or be poverty stricken. If perception was reality, all signs pointed to me being a typical statistic. Single parent household, abused as a child, two brothers incarcerated with life sentences, didn't finish college... yeah everything screamed, "You will FAIL". However, my thoughts at the time were, "I can do anything I put my mind to...". There was a certain level of fierceness and invincibility in me that I really can't describe. Maybe it was the motto that I was trained to speak out loud by my elementary school teacher, "I can LEARN, I must LEARN, my mind is a PEARL! I can do ANYTHING in the WORLD!".

Or perhaps, it was my History teacher, Mrs. Hollenbeck, at a high school I attended in Memphis, TN. She poured into me and told me how special I was and gifted with my words. She entered me into a NAACP Oratory contest, and I won 2nd place, but truthfully it felt like 1st place! Why? Just because she believed in me. Whatever the reason for the confidence, I embraced it and welcomed it!

Reflection: Have you experienced, or are you at a turning point in your life? What has been the wake-up call for you?

Monique or Becky: A Lesson in Voice Altering

My mother was a jack of all trades. I mean the true definition! She taught herself how to do nails and she would do the nails of every neighbor in our community. She also worked 9-5 in maintenance, as a leasing agent, did hair, sold candy, and even had fish fry Fridays. I remember coming home from school and there would be a long line of folks outside of our door waiting for their fish plate. Hindsight being 20/20, I think back on all those jobs she had and I believe they were prepping her for something greater. Yes she was skilled at all of those trades but it was purposed for her preparation.

My mom started her tax and accounting business in the 90's; it started off slow but very steady. She quickly became the "tax lady" on the southside of Atlanta. Eventually when she left her job and focused in on her business 100% it grew into a steady stream of income that afforded us the ability to move out of the hood into a "not so great but not so bad" neighborhood. My mom was a natural "hustler". She could sell water to a whale. Her tax business was lucrative but only lasted during the tax season. On top of that she was a single mom with kids, so she had to figure out something.

Her solution was starting a bathroom attendant service. In the late 90's, Buckhead was the premier spot to party in Atlanta. Not only was it the hang out, but it was in the predominantly white area. She proposed her idea to some of the owners to create a true luxury experience for their patrons by having her service in the bathrooms during evenings and night shifts. She made decent income doing this! I remember when I turned 15 she included me in helping with her businesses. In the bathroom attendant business, there were these party goers, and they would tip my mom but with me they would over compensate. Saying things like, " Oh my goodness, you are so pretty are you mixed with something else?" OR You can't just be black!" AND "Here's $20 stay in school, you don't want to end up here forever." Almost as if I asked them to give me some advice. This was my first experience of other races assuming that my beauty was not connected with my blackness but somehow that if I was mixed with something else, this would validate why I was beautiful. Once I caught on to their slightly prejudice comments, I would answer them by saying "Yes, I am mixed with black and blacker". Just watching their reactions would be enough satisfaction for me.

Nonetheless, this didn't stop in corporate America. Instead of the mixed questions, it would be the questions pertaining to touching my hair when it was curly versus when it was straight. I would get a different response from colleagues when my hair was in its naturally curly state. "Can I feel it?" or "Why on earth do you wear weave if you have hair already?" and my favorite was when they just walked up and touched it saying, "Oh I've always wondered how this hair feels" My reply, "Please, don't", was written all over my face.

Nonetheless, I was prepared for these instances simply because my mother exposed me to different cultures. She taught me how to react and manage different races of people but still stay true to who I am.

When I worked for her tax company she gave me the script on what to say when I picked up the phone, "Always include your name and the business along with how may I help you?" she would say.

I tried it, but I tried it using my regular Monique voice. My mom looked at me sternly and said, "No when you are talking to my clients, you need to switch it up." She answered the next call in the most professional voice. She enunciated her words, she spoke properly and even sat up straighter. It was like her whole demeanor changed.

That's when I recognized that I couldn't just be the same Monique that I was with my home girls, or even at home with my sisters or brothers. No, when I wanted to be professional, I had to alter my voice slightly and become a business oriented Monique. I switched it up not only for my mom's small businesses, but also when I went job hunting for part time gigs after school. My friends at the time were not impressed by my new found code switching. I remember one of my friends saying, "Monique will get in front of the manager, and I don't know if it's her or Becky talking."

I laughed with them but I knew that it was the polished demeanor that allowed me to receive rapid promotions. You see what they didn't realize was I truly was code switching around them as well. I preferred speaking intelligently and engaging in deep conversations with coworkers about life experiences. I would attend the meaningless night club events or lend a listening ear to the boy trouble with friends, but that was not completely Monique, just my adapted version of myself for them!

Reflection: Have you mastered altering your voice or speech patterns to fit various scenarios and environments? How does it make you feel?

Who Me? (Receiving Criticism)

In my work behaviors and ethics, I've always been described by colleagues as a perfectionist. Nowadays, I would have to say I'm still a bit hard on myself, but I don't allow it to affect relationships around me or stress me out. I became that way because my mom was a beast in her work life. She thrived in delegating and coordinating projects for her many businesses and events. Naturally, I grabbed some of her work ethic.

In one of my previous positions, I was praised almost monthly. I had an insane work ethic. I came in early. I worked my tail off, worked virtually 2-3 days, and I had a team of two ladies (right out of college) that reported to me. I trained them to do everything I knew how to do. I loved that position! Eventually change occurred, the company was acquired and the culture went from happy and fun to cold and distant. After the acquisition, I stayed as long as I could and then moved on. Eventually, I came to a completely virtual recruiting company that needed sourcers.

They were absolutely the perfect fit for me in terms of flexibility. I considered myself the BEST because I enjoyed what I did and I understood sourcing and recruiting. So adding that confidence with my history of compliments and praises my entire career, equaled a BIG HEAD!

Coming into the team I didn't feel quite connected. I felt like I was being watched as if to say let's see if she will win or fold in this environment. I must admit it was a great team, and they were the best sourcers I'd ever worked alongside.

Eventually, I had my first performance review and my manager was this very cool outspoken, but comical California lady. Let's call her Charlie. She says, "Yeah, Mo we think you have some really great potential but here's some areas you need to improve…" I'm thinking, "Improve? Who me? Is she crazy? I'm perfectly fine! This job is less than I was making in my previous position what is her problem??". I say, "Well, I guess you are entitled to say that..."

Charlie continues, "Yeah it's not just that. You think you are expert level in every area but you're not... Here's the thing, you don't know everything Mo."

That was it! After she gave me that feedback, I was ready to quit! I began cleaning up my LinkedIn profile and notifying my network that I was exploring options.

The calls and emails started coming in to explore new opportunities… but guess what? She was right!!

I was so full of myself that I wouldn't even think about the fact that her criticism of me was on point and constructive she just didn't quite say it as tactfully as she could have said it. I did what I knew best which was to leave. In my brain I thought, "I'm sticking it to you now because I'm gone and you need to figure out how to replace me. So long! "

I did not see that she was merely trying to bring out a better version of me. She had poured into me and tried to help me succeed by pushing me to host training calls and matched me up with a mentor to support me in areas that I needed help. But because I let compliments and praises affect my view of myself, I left from under her wing and ended up in a position making almost the amount I was accustomed to making with all sorts of perks but (you knew there was a but coming didn't you), no one poured into me. There was no real training; my manager barely connected with me to develop my skills or even ask about how my days were going.

I can remember presenting idea after idea even going to others in leadership to propose my ideas for my team and him denying them. I have always been social media savvy and tried implementing social media into my responsibilities and his answer to me and others was, "Monique just needs to focus on I.T." The irony of it all was during my final performance review before he was slated to leave the company, he gave me a 3 (satisfactory) in all areas but a 2 (needs improvement) in driving results because he said I was too ambitious in my personal career coaching business and not the company's. Instead of being argumentative I simply replied, "Thank you for feedback I don't agree but I understand and appreciate it."

I learned my lesson then, that God vindicates me I don't have to lay down and be walked over but I also didn't need to fight over every area that I don't agree with.

However, it brought it all back to the Manager that I had before him that actually wanted to pull more out of me and put me in position to do more. Sometimes we have to learn to appreciate the position we are in before we can go to the next level or next position. We have to iron out those pieces within us that are not satisfactory so that we don't carry that on to the next point in our career. You can't leave when the going gets tough. If you are desiring to leave you must make sure you identify hurt if any and resolve it before you head out. Otherwise, that hurt will follow you to the next place.

You may not be as stubborn and prideful as I was. You could be desiring to move because you and your manager just don't seem to see eye to eye. Or he/she may not be supportive of your development. Or the leadership is close-minded and not understanding of your ambitions. Even if you're leaving because of the above mentioned, just identify your flaws first. Then I want you to tackle them! If it's caused you to slack on your job, stop and get back into beast mode. If hurt has caused you to disengage or ignore your colleagues and managers, then switch it up and act in love! The sooner you fix the hurt and react to it with positivity, the sooner you can create a far more effective exit strategy.

Take a moment to reflect: Have you been so anxious to leave a position based solely off of hurt or criticism? Did you take the time to evaluate yourself and your attitude? What were your results?

_____

_____

_____

_____

_____

_____

_____

_____

_____

_____

_____
_____

Appearance & Presentation

Respect the Code Law #1, "Change your environment, change your life"

So picture this. A brown girl that's normally accustomed to other brown folks with a true poverty "crabs in a barrel" mindset, females picking a fight simply because she spoke differently, abusive childhood, low self worth and esteem. With all of this baggage and obstacles she moved to Boston, MA believing that she was destined for greatness.

That brown girl was me. I am the girl that moved from College Park, GA to Boston, MA only knowing my Aunt! Now that's changing your environment

Living in Boston, MA there were so many different girls and guys that looked like me but they were Dominican, Haitian, or Cape Verdean. And believe it or not I was accepted and befriended almost instantaneously by each type of culture. I didn't encounter one bad experience while in Boston, MA. I am not saying that there weren't bad environments. I am saying my environment and who I chose to connect with were positive and inspiring people.

My roommate was my Russian "bestie" named Sophia and she helped me understand that no matter what language you spoke, whether you came from a small town in Georgia or a small town in Russia the goal was to be a success. The end game was to be successful!

I enjoyed learning about myself especially through my circle at the time. Coming from the south, there were words that I couldn't say properly. (I laugh now just thinking about them) One word was "ask". I would say, "Hey, let me axe you a question" my friend would say no. I would say "Why not?!" He'd say, "You may not AXE me anything because I don't want you chopping me up!" It literally took me about 2 minutes to understand but after I did I was so embarrassed!

Environmental conditioning is an incredible thing. Most of the teens that grew up around me spoke in broken English, slang, and improper dialect but it sound so normal to me at the time. I didn't even realize my AXE was a proper speaking person's ASK. Even now, I work hard to watch my dialect and how I pronounce things in meetings and speaking engagements. I'm saying this to a reader that is currently nervous about how you speak in front of corporate professionals or intellectuals. I am here to tell you "You can change your environment and it will change your LIFE!"

Place yourself around different people, continue reading awesome books (written by me of course), and ASK a person you respect to grade your speaking skills. You will change for the better, just be consistent.

Effective Communication can make or break your success level. What are interpersonal skills you learned that proved vital to your development?

_____

_____

_____

_____

_____

_____

_____

_____

_____

_____

There are times when looks can be deceiving. Sometimes I prematurely used my gift to help others who weren't necessarily ready to receive. I remember one time seeing a friend from high school at my brother's graduation. She actually worked at the stadium as a ticket person. Here's how our conversation went down:

Me: Oh my goodness "Sasha"! It's so good to see you!

Sasha: Thanks girl you look great!

Me: Thank you thank you! What have you been up to?

Sasha: Just working. Trying to maintain.

Me: Ok so is this your part time gig?

Sasha: No this full time.

Me: Girl, you were always super smart in school. What else are you wanting to do for a career?

Sasha: (stares for a second) Well I... I don't know I just am trying to pay bills.

Me: Oh no no no! We gotta get you a better position, you are smart enough to do whatever you want!

Sasha: (looks offended)

Me: I'm not saying there's anything wrong but I'm a recruiter, and if you want I just would like to help you get a better position.

Sasha: Look, I'm good but thanks, I gotta go.

Me: (Mouth opened, standing outside of the stadium, wondering what I did wrong.)

As I share this story I laugh. Not at her feelings being hurt or offended, but at my true naïveté of what she was upset about. I truly thought in my heart that I was being helpful! I can even remember the car ride home thinking how rude and ungrateful she seemed.

Here's the thing, she couldn't be ungrateful for something she did not ask for. It's ok to be a game changer and desire to change the world. However COMMA (that comma is emphasized on purpose) it's not ok to try and change someone's predicament if they are not soliciting your advice or assistance. Especially not on what it looks like to you or what you think their life appears to be. There were several things that could have been going on with her:

1.) She is perfectly happy and I was just over analyzing her appearance

2.) She is married and just working to have extra income because her spouse is the breadwinner

3.) She is going to school to finish a bachelor's or even a masters and needs to work non traditional first shift hours.

I'm sure you could make some educated guesses on what it could be. But truth be told, I don't know what her situation is or was at that time. The only thing I know is this:

You cannot judge a book by its cover. You also cannot offer unsolicited advice based on your own perception of someone else's life. RESPECT THE CODE! Open your mouth when someone requests your knowledge or advice about personal things.

Have you ever experienced a moment in your past where you judged a person too soon? Perhaps offered some unsolicited advice based upon the appearance of someone vs the reality?

Write down the biggest lesson you've learned from that experience.

_____
_____
_____
_____
_____
_____
_____
_____
_____
_____

Video Vixen Body, Oprah Winfrey Mind

Basically, being curvy stuck out like a sore thumb in corporate America. Women of all shapes and colors would make comments to me about being "thick". Many others just sneaked a peek as I walked by.

Now in the 'hood, or the south side, I was praised for my shape.. Almost honored because it was "natural" or without surgery. Some would say, I had the shape that many of my friends and some celebrities were paying for.

After awhile I just bought into the hype and decided to embrace it. As a woman of color, with a go getter attitude, great work ethic and a "curvy" shape… I wasn't someone that the corporate arena could easily forget. Believe it or not I was judged by my shape throughout different times in my career. Some would insinuate that because my body is curvy that I couldn't hold a decent or intelligent conversation. Some would say things in shock such as "Wow that's a great statement!" or "Where did you hear that from?"

You may be thinking, well you have to wear certain types of clothing when you have a shape like that. The "shape like that" comment would get me so angry when I was a less experienced, young corporate woman. I felt that I should be able to wear whatever I desired to wear at work. Well you know the saying, "hindsight is 20/20".

At one very huge communication company, I was an Executive Assistant. I was the youngest one on the team. The lead EA put me in mind of that "Yes suh No suh" older woman in the movies. She and I clashed often. She pulled me to the side one day and decided to coach me on my work outfit. Now it was the exact same outfit that a Caucasian colleague had purchased from Express. It was a pencil skirt and a fitted collar shirt. I felt invincible and very executive in this outfit. I gave, (let's call her "Mabel"), a piece of my mind; very tastefully. My response was, "Well I don't recall you being HR… and furthermore it doesn't show anything… no cleavage and the skirt goes to my knees, what do you want me to do? wear a robe? "

Mabel looked at me and said in a whisper, "I get what you're saying but ok …just trying to help… I've been around the block a few times and I know what's respected."

I said, "Respect? I finish my work, manage his calendar, do all his expense reports and I come over to help you because I finish my work in half the time you do.. Suzie wore the skirt two weeks ago and received compliments. So again, why wouldn't they respect me when I'm not showing anything and I do my job?"

Mabel looked me dead in my eyes, "They won't ever respect you if you wear shape fitting clothes on a body like yours. You're not Suzie"

She picked up some extra lunch boxes that she stopped by my desk to get and walked away.

Not too far away, I looked at Suzie walking into the break room, blonde hair, tiny frame, no backside curves whatsoever. Smiling confidently and having small talk with various individuals as she walked. She was respected, admired and culturally accepted. I knew I didn't want to be Suzie but I wanted to feel what it was like to just BE in her shoes. I remember walking in that same area to that same breakroom and barely getting eye contact from the team I served daily. And as angry as I was with Mabel, I knew she was right to a certain degree. However, I didn't want to learn quite yet. I was still young and rebellious! I wasn't ready to RESPECT THE CODE! I thought if I made more money and appeared successful or at least a higher level than an EA, THEN "these people" would have no choice but to respect me! So I started looking for work again.

As I encountered more professional women in corporate America, I noticed that there were just some that were taken seriously and there were others who were not. Alot was based upon their skills, demeanor, and guess what else? You guessed it! Yes, their work attire.

Now, the demeanor was easy I was a mixture of dominant and compliant personality factors. Which meant that I can shine easily in a leading role BUT I knew how to follow when necessary. I kept abreast of the latest trends to make sure my skills were up to par. My wardrobe changed as I understood what I wanted to be a representation of me in a corporate environment. I made up in my mind that I wanted to be taken seriously and carried myself that way every day.

My best teacher was my first real deal boss "Ms. Leanne", she was the staffing agency's branch manager. Boy it was hard winning Ms. Leanne over. She was such a tough cookie. I remember her dress code was conservative business corporate, which meant blue, black, gray or neutral colored suit. You could not wear anything sheer, too tight, or skirts 1/2 inch above the knee. Her biggest rule ever, was NEVER ever come to work without wearing pantyhose. Yes panty hose! No matter if it was rain, sleet, snow, or sunshine.

One morning, I was rushing and risking almost being late. So I thought to myself, "*Hey I've been here 4 months I don't have to wear pantyhose stockings every day, besides I've got on pants not a skirt.*" I remember thinking that I could get none over on her because she stayed at her desk a majority of the morning. I ran into the morning meeting first so Ms. Leanne couldn't see that I did not have on pantyhose. As I am rushing out after the meeting was over, she stops me and says, "You're either professionally dressed or you are not. You have two choices, you can go home without pay or you can put some stockings on within the next 10 minutes." I started to tell her my excuse. She interjected and repeated, "Two Choices."

I went to my desk and my heart was racing. I can remember running to Vee and asking her what I should do because Ms. Leanne was going to fire me. She laughed and said, "Girl, go get you some pantyhose!" The light went on in my brain and I remembered there was a corner store exactly 4 minutes walking distance if I ran to the corner store that was near our block in the heart of Midtown, Atlanta I could change in the bathroom and be back in the office in 10 minutes. So I ran like my life depended on it and accomplished everything in 10 minutes. Ms.Leanne came up to the front never even looked at my shoes, barely looked at me and asked me to bring her the morning batch report for the payroll.

I didn't understand at the time, but Ms. Leanne was grooming me to Respect the Code with my attire. She paved the way for my thought process to mirror her own. Her mindset was, if you are going to be in a conservative setting where businesses paid her branch hundred thousands of dollars to find superstar talent, she had to make sure that you looked like a million bucks. It did not matter to me at that point what type of shape I had, I just had better get IN SHAPE or I was out of a job. She may have been the best boss I've ever had.

Take a moment to reflect, have you ever worn something too tight, too revealing, or lacking grooming in a corporate environment? Why do you believe you wore it? And how did it make you feel?

_____
_____
_____
_____
_____
_____
_____
_____
_____
_____
_____
_____
_____
_____
_____
_____

Interview: Research & Proposals

I have always been very competitive. I like to win. In my past, I felt like I had so many losses growing up that my eagerness to prove myself showed up in the interview.

After I was inspired to change part time careers I remembered driving past a Modeling & Acting Center. I thought to myself, "I would love to work there." Scout talent and book modeling & acting gigs sounded like a dream. In my past I had done some modeling and felt I knew what was in and what was not. I researched the director of the center.

Researching at that time, was yahoo searching the internet to find information. I looked up myspace and every internet search engine. I came up with a little information and found her email and sent her my resume (that I created from scratch focusing on modeling and being customer service friendly) in the email I expressed what I thought she wanted to hear:

"Hi Toula How are you? I am an actress /model that has had one on one coaching and training as well as success in the modeling arena with various ads, fashion shows, and campaigns. I have a true passion for modeling & acting and would love to work for such a prestigious modeling acting center as this one. My dream job is to be a talent agent and help match actors and models with gigs that they love! Do you have a moment to chat with me this Wednesday or Friday? It wouldn't take more than 10 minutes of your day."

That was it! I created an intro email just by sharing with her what I assumed a great employee of her establishment would look like. I didn't make the email long and drawn out. Just straight to the point. The conclusion of my email I asked for what I wanted. A phone or face to face conversation. Well, she accepted the invitation. I received a phone call and an in-person invite. And of course I got the job.

While at this position I learned so many things about myself:

- I could never meet a stranger
- People listen (really listened) when I spoke
- I have the gift of persuasion
- I desire to help others more than I like to get a sale!

Believe it or not there are tons of individuals who enjoy interviewing. I happen to be one of them. I've always felt a rush about winning someone over with my skills and experience. My interview skills developed as the level of my positions increased.

I mentioned earlier one of the best bosses I've ever had, Ms. Leanne. I remember back in the day coming into her staffing company after I just had my son. I was a single mom, young and eager to prove myself. I came to interview for an executive assistant role. My background consisted of me being in a receptionist or administrative role at that time. The EA position paid $25 an hour and seemed pretty easy. I researched the attributes of a great Executive Assistant and mentioned every point during the job interview. (Researching has always been a strategy that seemed to work in my favor.) Well the young woman that interviewed me was so impressed that she wanted me for the staffing agency's recruiting coordinator position instead of the executive assistant role. She was a pretty lady, business sharp, knowledgeable and you can tell she was one of the best and on her game. It was something about her that I connected with. Let's call her Vee.

She was super convincing about the staffing agency's position and had asked me to come back for a second interview. She explained to me that this position could easily lead to being promoted to a recruiter position. I wasn't all that familiar with what a recruiter was at that time, but I was happy to give it a shot.

"Listen you are perfect for this role and I'm ready to hire you but… it's just one person that you have to get pass and she's the manager over this branch. She really loves the current recruiting coordinator we have now "Joselyn" but Joselyn is relocating to another state. So just show her everything you showed me the day I interviewed you". Vee said this with a hint of worry that I could detect.

Even in noticing her nerves show up a little, I was excited. Why? Because I loved a challenge. Selling myself came naturally because I always felt I had something to prove. Now I wasn't sure if that was a good thing or a bad thing, but I knew it is a talent that I needed to possess.
So I met with the branch manager, Ms. Leanne who was a tiny lady that had a powerful presence. She wore a crisp clean business suit and a short haircut.

Ms. Leanne had a no nonsense look on her face and as soon as she sat down she looked at her watch. As if to say, "You've got 5 minutes to prove that you are not a waste of my time." However, I took it as I have 5 minutes to see if this is a manager that I want to work for. She asked me the toughest questions and I hit her with sharp answers. It was fun, I was direct to the point without seeming to be overly confident. She ended with, well we have a couple more candidates to interview and then we will let you know.

She made me wait, but she selected me.. And I got my start at a staffing agency as a recruiting coordinator.

In most corporate interviews you must **Respect the Code Law #2: "Do your research".** How can you provide the answer to a company's need if you don't know what they actually need? Respecting the Code in the interview means knowing the job, understanding the hiring manager, and maybe even some intel on what happened to the previous person in the position you are applying for.

For example, in today's time I visit glassdoor.com and review the company's mission & vision. As well as find reviews that pertain to the company's interview style and culture. This information can also be very valuable to creating a 90 day proposal. A 90 day proposal is your way of telling a potential employer that you take this position with their company serious. It shows that you have identified bottlenecks in the first interview and you desire to develop a solution plan to solve them.

Now for me, my 90 day proposal was absolutely mandatory for a 2nd interview. In my proposal, I solved the issues and the obstacles that the hiring manager/recruiter mentioned in the first interview.

My proposal tackled those areas of improvement in my first 90 days. It's all about visualization with hiring managers. It's not good enough to tell them you are a good fit, you have to make them see you in their positions!

Here's how I broke my proposal plans down

- Title of Strategy
- What strategy is designed to close the gap of
- Description of Strategy
- Possible Tactics
- Action Items
- Time frame per each item

Let's take some time to reflect. What role do you see yourself in next? What are some great 90 day proposal ideas that you can implement for your next position?

_____

_____

_____

_____

Having your 90 day proposal is only half of it. You must actually know how to implement those action items. Do your research. I've seen countless professionals hear about a 90 day proposal, add it to their interview and pitch for the position, and then bomb the first 90 days with a termination letter included because they couldn't dish out what they were selling.

It's important to understand that it is difficult to get to the top within corporate America without sacrifice and being teachable. Sacrifice hours and hours of doing what you want to do, and do what you need to do in order to be considered an expert in your field.

Are you going to the networking events in your industry? Are you volunteering or offering your skills to a non profit organization? All these things are great for you to experience but they are also great to help hone into your skill set.

Get & Maintain the Job

Ok you interviewed well and now you've been offered the job. Well, I am all about making sure the salary, work outcome, and environment matches my values, passion, and personality. Hopefully you will learn to see the significance in filtering each job you seek through your values, passion, and personality. As a Career Coach, if there's one thing I've learned, it's that Career Coaching is not just for individuals in transition or unemployed. A good Career Coach shows you how to maneuver through various obstacles in a corporate arena while strategizing how to achieve your career aspirations and goals. First things first, pull out the 90 day proposal that you promised to achieve and start dissecting everything you proposed. Make sure you don't bite off more than you can chew.

Work Esteem and Self-Motivation
Respect the Code Law #3: "Build your own work esteem, don't wait on others to build it".

Attaining specific goals in your job will assist you in promotion. You want to make sure you are respecting the code by knowing your managerial environment. What does that mean? It means learning how to stay in your lane. In my experience, I've learned that managers are humans too. And just as the most confident and secure manager can see the strengths and rockstar capabilities in you, so can a manager who may not be as confident and perhaps somewhat insecure. The aforementioned manager may want to groom you, push you towards success, and even be a little harder on you than your other colleagues because of the greatness identified within you.

The latter manager may attempt to block you from certain opportunities to shine or withhold your praises. I'm all too familiar with each of those extremes because I have experienced them both. On one hand, I had to learn and ACCEPT that the confident leader that I had only wanted the best for me. She (Ms. Leann), pushed me like there was no tomorrow, genuinely rewarded me when I outshined others, opened the door for my new ideas, and allowed me to learn more of what she did daily. Now at the time, I was not ready to receive that type of grooming. I wanted to make a lot of money and instead of sticking around and being groomed by Ms. Leeann, I decided I would follow the money and be an Executive Assistant at a huge corporation. I enjoyed the position but it was missing the mentorship that I subconsciously loved, the fast paced environment of the staffing agency, and the competitive atmosphere.

It's funny how walking out of your lane and jumping into someone else's lane because of money, can lead you down a path of mistakes one after the other. I don't want to digress but let's just say, I continued chasing the money instead of filtering jobs through my personality, values, and passions. I only saw one thing: INCOME. Meanwhile, I would just keep running into managers/supervisors instead of leaders. They would watch my hours, tell me if and when I made mistakes but never truly had a desire to draw greatness from me. I remember learning that one of my managers said, "I don't want someone to come here and have new ideas and suggestions. I just want a worker bee." When you are under "leadership" like that your first reaction is to just allow things to fall into place. Do the minimum and keep your ideas to yourself. But you have to push pass that feeling.

There are ways to RESPECT THE CODE within a hostile environment without losing your ingenuity. I remember not too long ago, being in a very toxic environment. The company had some of the best perks but treated their employees solely like dollar signs. There were little to no tools to do our jobs, no professional development, or mentorship. Other concerns included no commission structure (even after it was promised), change of leadership time after time, no true assessment of the current staff's abilities besides a resume, inadequate ATS system, and unbalanced metrics. There were new ideas not received unless you were related to a person in power or a non-minority. It was just a nightmare. My work esteem had dropped considerably low.

Yes, there is work esteem just as much as there is self-esteem. Imagine being told no to every idea you propose but another person of a different race has the exact same idea and gets the yes. Or imagine your leadership changing multiple times but still no one leading you. Imagine being hired as a virtual employee but being told you are not eligible for promotion because you are a virtual employee.

Here's the thing, low work esteem can affect the brightest most talented workers and the mediocre ones as well. In lieu of my confidence of my work becoming lower due to leadership, I chose to blend in and just do my job.

This consisted of me just doing the duties I was asked to do but nothing more or less. However, that choice was not very beneficial to my growth. I am a mover and an innovator by nature, and if I'm not growing then I'm not learning and being utilized to my fullest capabilities. Eventually, I began to stop waiting for recognition from my leadership. Instead, I serviced my clients and candidates by pouring everything into them. I brought my customer service and client service from a 6 to an 8. This included making myself available to career coach my employees into better positions and more money, creating a newsletter recognizing my employees and inviting them to networking events. I made myself available to offer training to my colleagues that asked me for it. I spent lots of nights praying and believing that God desired more for me. That he would be my vindicator, my promotor, and my elevator… not man. A couple of months of me making that shift happen in my mind, quickly in real life I was receiving recognition all over the place. I made a goal in my mind to change the way our current clients and associates viewed us within my division. Although I respected the code of the environment being a non-welcoming one for new ideas and innovation from me, I was still able to shine and help colleagues and employees shine by shifting that energy into different parts of my job.

Time to reflect: Have you ever had your goals and plans totally shifted from what you thought you were going to be doing? Did your work esteem get affected? Were you able to remain positive?

Competing against myself not you

A little competition can't hurt anyone. As a matter of fact, there's nothing wrong with a little bit of healthy competition. I know for me, it's a part of my personality. I am a healthy competitor. If I see someone in my lane doing a better job than I am doing I raise my standards and decide to produce better results than I have previously. I guess you can say in a sense, I am competing against myself and not anyone else. We do have to be careful when Respecting the Code has the potential to go wrong. If you are in a highly competitive atmosphere and that's not your natural nature, you may end up doing things that will manipulate your win versus naturally winning fair and square.

In one of my positions, there was this really nice but passive aggressive older lady. She pretended, more often than not, to play dumb in order to get smart. Her true nature was education prior to coming into the staffing and recruiting business. She was not naturally competitive but because of the nature of the beast in staffing she became more competitive. She and I did not hit it off at first; she was not culturally sensitive and asked inappropriate questions as well as comments. She irked me more than I should have let her but, during this time I detached myself. I felt like a zombie. I was consumed with not being treated fairly and not feeling apart of the team. I worked and kept my head down. I considered myself a loner. But the truth was, the way I was designed by our Creator, was to be outgoing and extroverted. My work esteem and my value continued to fall lower and lower. I could not stop the thought running through my mind of how unfair I was treated. But then I started fighting back with positive affirmations all over my office just as I did when I was younger. (Sometimes we have to remember the same things that got us out of stinking thinking can do it again!)

I began speaking them out loud. I remembered a book I had purchased titled *40 Days of Biblical Declarations* by Kimberly Jones, and I said positive declarations out loud everyday! I began to not hold my colleague's actions against her after discovering more about her through conversation. I understood that we were not in competition because the playing field wasn't even. I realized that I had a much more formidable player to compete against: Myself.

I worked hard, and made my clients happy and my employees happier. I pushed myself and recognition eventually came but by then I had already made up in my mind that I was created to do more than just a 9 to 5.

Resting !@$#% Face

The only person that can stop you, is YOU. I noticed a long time ago, that a lot of successful women with dominant personalities had this distinct stigma. No matter how we Respected the Code with our attire, our attitude, or even our language, there was one thing that we could not hide unless we tried: The Resting Mean

Face. (I've taken the liberty to change the name a bit, but you know what "mean" is replacing.) It's not always because we have an attitude or even a mean persona. Sometimes, it's simply because we are thoughtful and somewhat internalize or digest the information we are receiving with our face.

Here's a test. So you are currently reading this book right? Take a moment to leave your face exactly where it is and take your cell phone out. Open up the camera, turn it to selfie mode and take a picture. If the picture looking at you looks like you have an attitude or perhaps you look like something is wrong, then your face may need to learn how to RESPECT THE CODE of the environment and setting that you are in.

For instance, while at a board meeting I was the only woman of color in the room. This was the norm for me at that point in my career. So I am intently listening to each word being said. The speaker, looks at me and asks, "what's wrong, what's on your mind?" Now truth be told, I was simply just listening to him and digesting what he was saying and he just so happened to catch me looking probably very unpleasantly at him. Now feeling pressured, I felt that I needed to come up with something quick. I needed to figure out what would be a better way to answer him besides, "Nothing's wrong". So I just told the truth. "I am digesting and taking it all in." And he seemed pleased enough with the answer, smiled politely and moved on. Now to him and many others, my face probably looked intimidating, confused, perplexed, annoyed but the truth is, I was not either. I was truly just digesting his information and my face was telling the story of receiving everything. I've witnessed women and especially women of color be labeled as "attitude" or "unapproachable" because someone decided to assume something was wrong instead of asking.

Here's the thing, women of color are stigmatized for our strong features and then because we naturally have them we are so willing to alter them or make excuses in order for us to blend in with the crowd.

Respecting the Code does not mean we lose ourselves in someone else's code. We don't have to get lost in the sauce. But what we do need to do, is stand firm on how we present ourselves to others in the workplace, in ministry, no matter the color. If our Resting Mean Face offends, then why not be MINDFUL of it. Here's some tips on how to present a more pleasant face:

- Be cognizant of your environment and remember that your energy is being watched along with your face. (No matter your position)
- Digest the words being said to you but don't internalize them. These are just words, they are temporary and fade away.
- Smile or Smirk while engaged in conversation. Even if you have to think of something that makes you happy at the same time. Keep smiling until it becomes a real smile
- Remember the words that you may not like being spoken to you don't belong to you. So don't take ownership of them. Relate and Release!

I have even noticed that many will embrace the negative connotation that comes along with the Resting Mean Face. Believing that somehow being mean to our fellow sisters and brothers no matter the race, is considered cute or something to be proud of. **Let's make time for reflections:**

Face Check! What nonverbal face messages are you sharing with others? Do you believe it's helpful or harmful to how others perceive you?

_____
_____
_____

Tone and Communication

Respecting the office code is one that I've learned over time is ever changing. Why? Because your environment is a reflection on which code you are trying to respect. I believe that there are diverse people and personalities in every work place. With understanding that, you just have to be observant and borrow some discernment from God. One of the biggest problems in any corporate arena is communication. Our biggest form of communicating is through emails.

What do you think emails and text messages have in common?

- You can never truly know how someone will perceive your message.
- Establishing a tone in the message can be difficult
- Response times of messages may be viewed incorrectly

I'm sure you can think of plenty others. I know that there have been times when someone has misinterpreted your message or you have misinterpreted someone else's message. The question is, how do you prevent it? In my experience I've had managers whose personalities varied. For example, one of my favorite bosses simply emailed me at 8am and expected a response by

8:30 am. Now, she was direct and not passive aggressive. At 8:25 am she would be asking did I receive the first email. So one way I alleviated her anxiety was emailing her back as soon as she emailed me!

Let's say she emailed me a question: "Jane Doe did not receive her check and she has an expense receipt that we need to add to that. What's her status on the report and do you know if payroll already approved her expense reimbursement?"

My natural response would be to go find all the details and then respond with the answer. Well, not when you are under a micro manager. With a micro manager's personality, this is how you set up an answer:

"Hi Ms. Leeann, I am reviewing our batch report to make sure Jane's payroll was included. Also, I'm not 100% sure about her expense receipts but I'm going to research everything and get back with you within the hour."

Notice something? I hope you did! I addressed her with Hi even though she did not do the same for me. Also, I have immediate actions that I stated I was currently doing. I was honest, and told her I wasn't sure about the situation. Last, I didn't give a definitive time to answer. Instead, I mentioned that I would get back with her within the hour. That means I understand that I'm depending on others for information, and I am not going to say I can have an answer by a certain time but I can have an update at the least by that time frame.

Respect the Code Law #4: Do unto others in email as you would want an email sent to you.

Remember, the tone you receive does not have to be the one you give back.

I've had managers who I thought were passive aggressive managers. These were the managers that seemed pleasant enough when we were face to face but underlyingly held something against me. At that time in my life, I perceived them to be somewhat intimidated by my ambition or perhaps my recognition. I only saw them look for flaws after a leader would mention how great I was doing. For example, after I received recognition or a great recommendation from a client, the next day like clockwork I would receive an email from this manager. It would say something like:

"Monique did you notice on one of your requisitions, the word Technical Engineer was not capitalized? Please be sure to review each requisition in its entirety before posting on our site."

Now my knee jerk reaction would be to clapback with a jazzy response. I was thinking if you are managing 20 people who all have mistakes up the wazoo much bigger than my capitalization error, how can you make time for my small mistake but not theirs?

But then I noticed he would do it EVERY time I received accolades. And then I did a 30 foot view assessment. I took myself out of the moment and put on my big girl glasses and looked at the entire situation from both perspectives.

And I thought to myself, "It's easy for me to perceive him as being this passive aggressive manager that hates me. Or I can look at the variables involved from a higher level of thinking. He's more of an introvert and I appear to be more of an extrovert. I am strong with customers, clients and engaging others and he wasn't the best at it. I have an innovative mind set and he was very business process focused. All of these things were by no means bad personality traits, just different from a person in a human focused role and perhaps difficult for us to relate to one another. Not to mention he may not have been too happy with his boss. After considering these details, I did something that changed my life. Which leads me to a very important **Respect the Code Law #5: "Change your perception, change your LIFE!"**

I changed my views. I said to myself, "Maybe he just wants the best for me. When I'm getting accolades they make him look great! So he may want to make sure I look good across the board and identifying those small things will help me be better in the long run."

Here's the thing, this manager would turn down my ideas, rarely create opportunities to communicate one on one with me, and didn't offer any personal development specific to me. But I didn't hold on to it after I assessed myself and chose to change my perception in every way relating to him. I don't want you to think that all of a sudden I became naive. No, I just recognized him and chose to not internalize his issues as my own. In turn, I went from avoiding him, to accepting him and praying for him. That's how your life changes! When you can do ministry in the workplace, you are WINNING!

Let's definitely reflect on this! Tell me about a time when you felt slighted by your manager. What was your initial reaction? Did things ever get better? How would you have changed your reaction if you viewed things differently?

_____
_____
_____
_____
_____
_____
_____
_____
_____
_____
_____
_____
_____

Office Norms

Respect the Code Law #6: "Thou Shalt Abide by the Office Norms"

Respecting the office code is pretty hard when you aren't clear on what office norms are. An office norm is an understanding or common sense behavior in the workplace.

Here are some specific office norms to live by in the workplace:

- Don't throw your colleague under the bus!
    - Everyone makes mistakes, so when your team mate makes one don't feel you have to immediately run to your supervisor. Go to your coworker and address it then move on. (Unless it involves sexual harassment, unethical actions or discrimination)
- Learn how to pick up the phone!
    - When an issue arises, After the first 3 email exchanges, it's time to pick up the phone. No going back and forth. Just get to the root of it!
- Caps Locks are only for congratulating or celebratory emails.
    - All Caps when you're angry or pointing something out, appears rude & obnoxious. Be considerate to the receiver of the Email.
- Reply All
    - When someone announces something, don't feel the need to reply all. If it's genuine, Email the person one on one.
- Manager add in/cc:
    - When attempting contact, don't feel the need to cc someone's manager unless you have called 2x and sent 3 emails with no response.

- - Also, when e-meeting someone for the first time, try to ask a mutual connection to initiate the first email. Do not cc everyone connected.

- Knowing the best time to gossip!
  - The absolute best time to gossip is never! If a coworker starts off with "Well somebody told me that.." cut them off and say "No thanks somebody told you… not me"
- Don't Wear your heart on your sleeve
  - Be emotional on your own time. The baggage stays outside the office or keep it at home.
- Abbreviations
  - Don't use K for Ok. Or Thx for Thanks. This is not a text message and can be deemed as lazy or lacking intelligence.
- Solution oriented
  - If you are going to complain, be ready to come up with a solution or partner with coworkers on a team solution for the issue.
- Balance
  - Work Life Balance is essential. Being the first person there and the last person to leave doesn't mean you are the most productive. Sometimes it just means you are the most unhappy.

The Respect the Code office norms are essential to put in place in any work environment.

I am not saying that these rules apply to every office and every environment. But they apply to most. My recent Vice President would reply to me with K instead of ok and because it bothered me that he responded that way I found myself responding to him in that same manner. Then I did a self check and realized that no matter who it was I would remain professional in my email language. Don't let anyone take you off your throne! What does that mean? Well it means that you have to set the standard even if others are not.

Are there any office codes that you can add to the list? Which codes/norms have you found to be problematic and which ones beneficial in your experiences?

_____
_____
_____
_____
_____
_____
_____
_____
_____
_____
_____

Relationships

Building relationships are vital to your career success. There is no i in team for a reason. Your team can consist of individuals outside of your department as well as inside. The key to building relationships is to not come into the relationship with a one sided or alterior motive. When you connect with colleagues, truly figure out what their goals are and how you can help them attain them. Eventually it will come back to you for your good.

There are some relationships that are not appropriate for the workplace as well as some that are meant to strengthen you.

Hopefully this chapter will help you understand how to differentiate which relationships are healthy and which ones are simply learning experiences.

Kissed alot of frogs but not that one

I've had my share of guys that I've dated but the one thing I recognized early on in my career was, never get involved with a coworker or manager. However, it took this lesson to realize even befriending a person of the opposite sex hard to be dealt with caution. I recall befriending a male coworker early in my career. We were strictly platonic and one day he tried to kiss me while we were out on a lunch break. Horrified, I pushed him, said No and rushed out of the car.

There are certain topics that I will never bring up for discussion in the workplace because of this experience. Our conversations included detailed dating, politics, lifestyle choices, personal preferences of our ideal mates, and flattery. At the end of the day, any person can get caught up in visuals without considering the code of the environment. Our deeply personal conversations, encouragement of one another and the times we hung out all were misconstrued because we were in the workplace and not respecting the code. In the workplace, when you blur the lines it can be fuzzy trying to figure out what's acceptable and unacceptable behavior.

At the time I was dating and kissing a lot of frogs, but that was one frog I did not want to kiss. I did explain to him that I didn't "like" him in that manner but I thought he was super cool like a brother. He visually cringed and thanked me for not thinking he was an absolute crazy person. I wish I could say that we snapped back into a great friendship again. I did not report him to HR I could have but did not. Unfortunately, we never quite returned to being friends. When he found another job, we were distant associates at best.

My biggest lesson from that was there's no such thing as "innocent flirting" in an office environment. The law to remember is **Respect the Code Law #7: "Respect the Code of the Office, it will Respect you"** Also, I learned that before I'm an employee, a coworker, or a friend, I am a daughter of the Most High God! Now in my more mature years, I know the do's and the don'ts of the workplace. I'm married now with a beautiful son & daughter and not only do I Respect the Code of my workplace but I Respect the Code of my marriage. I'm glad that I have had every experience that I've encountered because I know how to help my children and others on what to avoid in their careers.

Inappropriate Communication

Some of you may be reading this and thinking but what about the situations that occur that are not miscommunications? What about the times where you are respecting the code but others are not?

Here's a story that comes to mind. One of my leaders called me into his office for a touch basis meeting. I oblige and get excited about bringing some ideas to the table. Well we start off talking about the work load and he shows me some projects he's rolling out soon. He begins to talk about his personal life and his divorce and I start feeling a little bit uncomfortable. Then he proceeds to ask me do I think he's a catch. I shrug my shoulders and just say "sure I don't think you would find trouble getting back out there!" At this point every red flag is up and he says "Yeah but someone like you would never date someone like me." Immediately I laugh out of sheer nerves and tell him that I had another meeting that I needed to go to. He seemed angry at my response. I was so disappointed, here I was thinking that I was called into a meeting to partner on strategies and he was trying to find out if he was dateable.

The next week, he went from being very responsive to my emails to not responding to me at all. I had to go to his office and peek my head in after a week without a response. In order for me to get a response I had to ask something that involved a group of individuals. This went on for months and then he was terminated for some other inappropriate things.

Unfortunately, this happens quite often to women in the workplace. The more ambitious you are, the more open you are to vultures aka predatory corporate men aka "corporate thugs". You just have to be strong and value yourself and believe that your work can speak for itself. As a result of this leader's inappropriate communication, I decided to simply work hard. Some may think that I should have reported it to the HR team.

I watched multiple women in my career report various types of uncomfortable instances to HR and not only were they blacklisted from moving up in the company, some of them were deemed "trouble makers" and had the stigma of causing trouble in the department. The problem is the trust factor between HR and the leaders. Sometimes, instead of HR being unbiased and influential, they are simply just revealing the confidential conversations that the employee divulges to them. Which in turn makes that employee a target for backlash.

So far in my career, I've yet to encounter a dynamic HR team that truly desired to create a center of excellence for both the employee and leadership. I can't speak for every HR department only my experience.

Every situation is different, here's some tips to speaking with HR that maybe helpful:

- Assess your HR department and discern if they are receptive of guidance on your issue (if it's sexual harassment or discrimination then you absolutely should go no matter if they are receptive or not)
- Know that your case will be talked about on what HR deems is a "need to know" basis. Which normally gets back to the leader or manager that you have an issue with.
- Be cognizant, that in some cases executives get special treatment. When they behave badly, their repercussions are normally not as severe and rarely documented properly. Most executives do not receive the consequences that you might be expecting. Instead, they get an early retirement or a "voluntary" resignation.

The Case of the Ex

Have You ever been in a bad relationship or breakup? Well, if not let me tell you what happens sometimes. You tend to look at every person that comes after him/her in the same light. Especially the flaws! The flaws are sometimes anticipated and the anxiety can be so intensified that even the glimmer of an old trait or behavior will send you running out the door!

The only thing about living in the past is, you never know what's ahead of you because you are walking forwards looking behind you. How can you even be a functioning human being if you can't see what's in front of you?

This can happen to good employees under bad leadership. The manager that yells instead of speaks, that points out flaws versus acknowledging wins, picks and chooses which team member gets personal development, and encourages division instead of unity. Those are just a couple of attributes of bad leadership. I'm sure you may know of worse examples. I just want to lay down the foundation of what it looks like being in a toxic work environment.

Here's the thing, just as an ex can haunt your true movement towards happiness with your future mate so can a toxic work experience linger into your future work life contentment. Which leads us to **Respect the Code Law #8: "Don't carry past offenses into your future"**

I've only had one truly toxic work environment in my life. Although the position was attached to this grand organization the technology and the resources to actually successfully do your job just was not there. I remember being patted on the back and congratulated for being affiliated with this organization and all I could think in my mind was "God help me I'm drowning." I was drowning in a sea of contradictions, unstable leadership, fraudulent leaders, no training, no processes, no personal development, and no one advocating for you because everyone was out for self. Transparent moment, I felt trapped and I was extremely unhappy. Fridays were not TGIF for me, they were just a small break until Monday. I dreaded waking up on Mondays and would literally fear Sunday coming around the corner. I compared it to a family member who went to jail only on the weekends. I thought at one time, this is how she must feel.

After our third leader within three years and much prayer, I finally understood that this was not a punishment for me but it was preparation. It was like an epiphany! The toxic environment taught me absolutely everything that I shouldn't do in a position. It taught me how to run my own business and how to treat my employees. The same way I learned how to identify the red flags in leaders, the gossiping coworker or the back stabbing team leads, I also recognized that I needed to see the flaws but respect the human. I understood how to confess my own professional flaws so that I can hit the reset button.

Yes you guessed it. This leads me to **Respect the Code Law #9: "Confess your flaws, Change your future"** My professional sins that I would admit to myself and my Creator were things such as, not quickly responding to an email, being short or impatient with someone, not contacting someone when I know that I needed to call them, treating certain colleagues better than others, strongly disliking my boss, and purposely not working to my fullest capability. Once I admitted them, I would sit and ask God to forgive me and give me the strength to hit reset and not react to anyone in the way I felt I was being treated by my manager. Viewing things in that light, I felt that it was a trickling effect. Every bad experience that I had, influenced me to magnify the smallest flaws in a co-worker and use that to distinguish who they were. However, confessing to myself and hitting the reset button gave me another chance to start fresh and be the best me. It truly helped me understand that every colleague deserved a reset button as well.

One day in one of my Career Coaching sessions a client was explaining to me about all his issues with previous managers and leaders and how as a minority in corporate America he was overlooked for a promotion several times. He explained how he believed that a lot of the times his colleagues seemed intimidated and not open to want him to progress in his role. I listened silently until he let it all out. Afterwards, I told him to create a list of every person that he believed ever wronged him, slighted him, or sabotaged him in a corporate environment. He said he would probably have page and pages full of them. I said "Ok, that's good take as much as you need."

During our next session he was very eager to share every list and every single instance where this list of people had wronged him. I asked him, "Do you trust me?? He looked perplexed. "Well I guess, I don't know, yes?" I said, "Do you trust that my job as a Career Counselor is to make sure you are given the best strategies to take you to the next level that God has ordained for your life?"

He immediately said, "Yes! I do." I told him to read every name out loud and bring to his mind the hurt or pain they caused and tell them outloud that you Forgive them for whatever the pain was. It was an emotional session. After we went through an extensive list I asked him to throw it away and never bring it up again. Even if those hurt thoughts tried to creep in his mind, that he should give it to God. That's something I do for myself and have used to help others.

Write down every person in Corporate America that you believe ever hurt you. After you make your list, Forgive.

_____
_____
_____
_____
_____
_____
_____
_____
_____
_____
_____
_____
_____
_____

Keep Your Friends Close & Co-Workers Closer

I learned rather quickly that having enemies in the workplace was not the best choice a minority woman could make. In addition to being the only person of color at times, I also would watch men with no experience come in and do a job I could do in my sleep. So after realizing the politics of corporate America, I discerned it's not how much you know sometimes it's just who you know. Which leads me to **Respect the Code Law #10: "Empower others and you will be empowered too"**? I've always experienced the Power of Unity in spiritual instances. When two or more gathered together I knew those prayers could move mountains. So I adopted my own unity collaboration with colleagues at work and especially with women. I empowered colleagues that were associates, friends, and foes alike. I did not discriminate. I realize that I was a movement by myself but I was a force when I combined efforts with other coworkers. I respected the code of teamwork truly making the dream work.

For example, when I witnessed a coworker go above and beyond I made sure I wrote a stellar write up on their performance. I didn't care if they did this for me or not. However, 80% of the time they would also do the same for me. I tried my absolute best to offer superb customer service to my new hires and my hiring managers.

As a result, sometimes I would receive a raving email saying how much clients enjoyed my work ethic and the entire experience I offered. Once I received a recommending email, I would simply reply *"Thanks so much for your compliment, it was truly a pleasure serving you. I love receiving compliments, but my manager would love them even more. Please share your feedback of my work with him at _____"*.

I can recall my manager (the same one that told me I was too ambitious), inform me that certain people did not care for me arranging myself to look good for managers. He even mentioned that my ambition can hurt me as much as I "think" that it's helping me.

The funny thing is, he coached my male counterpart at that same job in the exact same role much differently. He would tell him to go after being noticed more and go after jobs outside of our normal category more, and my colleague (unbeknownst that he had suggested the opposite with me) would share that with me.

My colleague had no idea that our manager would suggest him to go and "get it", but suggest to me that my "go getting", was looked down upon. I learned that if I was going to Respect the Code of Empowering others, then I would need to figure out an exit strategy from under this type of management style. Truth be told the organization decided to severe ties with him and it was back to learning a new leader again for me.

Have you ever experienced a double standard related to your work behavior? How did you react to it? Do you think now that you could empower others in the midst of it?

_____
_____
_____
_____
_____
_____
_____
_____
_____
_____
_____
_____
_____

I can not say that empowering others always worked in both parties' favor. As a matter of fact, there were few times that it did not work out as I planned at all.

Throughout my career the story that pops in my head, was of a person I was encouraged to connect with by a manager. I was new and barely knew my recruiting coordinator. One day, my manager asked me into a meeting and asked me to show the recruiting coordinator that I was accessible to her and to let her know that I was willing to give her any tips on becoming a successful recruiter. He also mentioned that she had a bad rep for being combative, and for me to be careful of how I came across. Well, with my ambitious nature and "captain save a coworker" attitude, I dove in head first to show her I cared. I asked her to meet with me about 2 weeks later, and when she came in she was her normal dry.

I said, "So "Ria" I just want you to know if you ever want to shadow me or if I can help you out with any sourcing/recruiting techniques I am absolutely available and able to do so. I started off as a recruiting coordinator, and I was so fortunate to have someone give me a chance. I'm all about paying it forward so just let me know how I can help!"

Ria smiled and said "Thank you so much I really appreciate that. It's been crazy trying to find my sister a job right now if you know of any places hiring nurses…let me know."

Immediately, I gave her a number to a dear friend of mine that was a manager over a Medical staffing agency. She graciously took it and went about her business.

An hour later that same leader that asked me to connect with Ria called me into his office. I was very excited to give him my update of what I believed happened between myself and Ria. I simply remember him hanging his head down low and saying, "She didn't take it well." "She actually mentioned that you were intrusive and treated her in a condescending manner, etc"

I was shocked. I was floored. I kept thinking, "God why on earth would she say those things? I only wanted to help!"

After that I gave her time to cool off. I went to work the next day, and I apologized to her. I apologized if my extension to be helpful offended her and told her that was not my intentions. She ignored my apology and ignored almost every email that I sent afterwards. This would have been fine if she was a colleague that I didn't need. However, she was a support professional for recruiting. Which meant she was handling onboarding, new hire orientation and other tasks.

Finally, I went to her face to face and told her that she was important to me, and I really needed her to respond for the support of the business. I think that may have made it worse. I eventually went to my manager and told him all that had been going on since the previous encounter. He told me he would speak to her and get things straightened out. After a while, things became somewhat normal. But here's the backstory that I didn't know at the time; turns out she had a Master's degree with a concentration in Human Resources and believed because of it she was automatically next in line to get the position I was hired for.

I definitely empathized with her but I didn't excuse her. Whether it was sabotage on her end or truly feeling hurt emotionally. She handled it completely inappropriately and did not Respect the Code of the work environment. Instead of leaving her baggage outside the office door, she carried that emotional baggage around for everyone to see. Soon after that, she was replaced by a very pleasant woman who also possessed degrees but was one word she was not, *teachable*.

In my experience with Ria, I realized that I can't decide to "mentor" or empower someone just because I heard it from someone else. No, I would need to feel led to or they would need to come to me and express an interest in my mentorship on their own. I want to help but also I intend on respecting the code of the environment I am in. I can't just go trying to help those who don't desire to change.

I can't be the only person who has ever experienced someone misinterpret your kindness. How did you deal with it?

_____
_____
_____
_____
_____
_____
_____
_____
_____
_____
_____

Entrepreneurship & Small Business

My entrepreneurial journey started in 2013 when I was laid off from my job. The company where I worked had outsourced all recruiting activity to India recruiters that worked for half my salary. This led me to get into entrepreneur beast mode. I started my career coaching & recruiting business. I learned so much in a short period of time. My biggest lesson was consistency. When you stay consistent you can find clients that are attracted to your specific niche, style, service or product. Don't be afraid to seek business coaching. You may be gifted within self employment attributes but try not to do everything on your own.

It took me 4 years to learn that i couldn't do my business on my own. Once I hired a freelance virtual assistant, social media manager, and graphics designer my business revenue doubled.

Career Assessment

So previously I spoke about a Career Assessment that I completed. This was no ordinary Career Assessment this was the Mother of ALL Career Assessments. Why? It factored in something that was very dear to me. My VALUES. Yes, I had various personality traits and strengths that were also included BUT my values were essential to my happiness in my career.

My career assessment showed me so much about me! Prior to my career assessment I had so many different ideas of what I could be, but I wanted something that was fulfilling all the way around.

This assessment showed me how to filter my job choices with my personality, interests, skills and values. Here's some things I learned about myself:

- I had a pioneering spirit which I learned God designed in me so that I would have no fear or hesitation in moving into new territories.
- I'm very creative and thrive in creative writing or visual arts.

- That in order for me to feel content, I have to be in an environment where I am helping others.

These were just a few things I confirmed by taking this assessment. But with taking the assessment I still had to Respect the Code. **Respect the Code Law #11: "Thou shall not lie while assessing oneself"** What does that look like? I am glad you asked. It means while assessing yourself, you are in an area where it's just you and no one there to influence your decisions. It means that you are being honest and transparent with all of your answers and receptive to hearing things about yourself that you may not want to hear. One way I like to suggest is, asking someone that you don't connect with often, "How would you describe me to someone that didn't know me?" WHEW! That answer will surprise and enlighten you.

I realized that certain personality traits that I thought were not so great, were actually perfect for who God designed me to be. That I could easily start a business, and influence others in a positive way that would ultimately help them in various areas of their lives. I was BORN to be an entrepreneur! I am a Dream Birther! It pushed me to start a group on facebook that I call, The D.O.P.E. method. It's where I push men and women to do what they are designed to do and to be DOPE while doing it. The acronym, Divine Operation in Purpose & Excellence, gave me the nickname #TheDOPEpusher. I love the play on words and it's exactly what and who I am.

Let's reflect on your Career Identity! Have you assessed yourself? Are you confident that you are in the role that you are designed to be in? If not, what elements are missing?

_____
_____
_____
_____

_____
_____
_____
_____
_____
_____
_____
_____

Small business still a business

Starting off your small business as a side hustle is not the easiest thing in the world. There are others who take an even harder walk and dive into full entrepreneurship. But either way starting is the most necessary thing in the world. Why? Because every dream has to start somewhere. My dream has always been to have my own training & staffing company where I help ex-felons, unemployed, and dislocated workers re-enter the workplace. I currently have the training part of my business down. My goals are coming to fruition but first I had to adjust my thinking in these areas:

<u>Time Management & Prioritization</u>:

- Remember the order of Priority is GOD, Spouse, family, work & ministry.
  - Remember that balance is key, so creating a spreadsheet with a daily task list of responsibilities that include family time is essential

<u>Exit Strategy</u>:

- Financial planning is important. Creating a financial pro forma will assist you in going after capital for your business.
- Knowing your X
  - Saving your X amount of dollars before telling your corporate job goodbye.
- Going out with a bang!
  - Completing those projects that you started in excellence

Stretching:

- God doesn't give you more than you can bear.
  - Even when my plate was full to the capacity, God continued to make a way. I was being stretched to handle more tasks at one time and walk in confidence.

Thankful:

- Be grateful for the small opportunities and the huge ones. Someone out there may not be receiving any opportunities at all.

Support:

- Familial support is mandatory.
  - Your husband or wife absolutely must be behind you in your exit of corporate america. There will be hiccups and growing pains. Stick with it!

Take a look at the above areas to implement. Did you notice the acronym? It's TESTS. Consider **Respect The Code Law #12: "Tests will lead to Testimony"**. There will be many tests and trials but you will discover exactly how to be the best entrepreneur ever by being consistent through them all and recognizing your testimony.

My taste of entrepreneurship has not been as in depth as my walk in Corporate America. However, after watching my mom do it for so many years, I am confident that I can take what I've gleaned from her along with the lessons I've learned in corporate and make something out of nothing! I can flip this thing and make money without compromising my values! And guess what? You can too!

Laws in Effect

I never claimed to know everything I don't even claim to be an expert contrary to what others may call me. But I do know how to make something out of nothing. I do know (after countless trial and error experiences how to successfully maneuver through corporate America. I do know how to come from a poverty stricken environment and neighborhood to thrive in an affluent atmosphere without even a college education.

What I did wasn't a huge secret or outlandish scientific formula. I just remained faithful to some very important Respect the Code laws. Let's stick with laws for a moment. What's the definition of a law? Well, I looked up the word law and it had multiple definitions. One being:

1. a statement of fact, deduced from observation, to the effect that a particular natural or scientific phenomenon always occurs if certain conditions are present.

The other definition also jumped out at me:

1. body of divine commandments as expressed in the Bible or other religious texts.

Now both of these definitions minister to my soul! So factual statements drawn to a conclusion from observation- if I do certain things follow certain rules, then a PHENOMENON will occur. Ok let's pause for a minute. Can you look at yourself in any mirror and say, "I AM a PHENOMENON!" Just so we are on the same page, here's the definition of a phenomenon:

1. a fact or situation that is observed to exist or happen, especially one whose cause or explanation is in question.

Ok so I'm going to put it all together in simpler terms. IF you follow the Respect the Code laws outlined in this book, a phenomenon will occur! You will be that phenomenon.

Another definition for phenomenon:

> 1. a remarkable person, thing, or event.

The laws and testaments from the Bible if followed sincerely will lead to a path of prosperity, fulfillment and happiness. Not to say that challenges won't arise but the end goal that can be achieved is success. Not success as the world believes but success from a Godly perspective.

When I tell you that God made everything that I did bad in my life, turn out for my good. I went from a dope boys girlfriend, to now a D.O.P.E MAN's WIFE. D.O.P.E. meaning Divine Operation in Purpose & Excellence. It's my trademarked method that I now use as part of my Career and Business coaching program. Believe me, everything happens for a reason.

Let's Recap the Respect the Code Laws

Respect the Code Law #1: "Change your environment, change your life"

Respect the Code Law #2: "Do your research"

Respect the Code Law #3: "Build your own work esteem, don't wait on others to"

Respect the Code Law #4: "Do unto others in email as you would want an email sent to you"

Respect the Code Law #5: "Change your perception, change your LIFE!"

Respect the Code Law #6: "Thou Shalt Abide by the Office Norms"

Respect the Code Law #7: "When you Respect the Code of the Office, it will Respect you back"

Respect the Code Law #8: "Don't carry past offenses into your future"

Respect the Code Law #9: "Confess your flaws, Change your future"

Respect the Code Law #10: "Empower others and you will be empowered too"

Respect the Code Law #11: "Thou shall not lie while assessing self"

Respect The Code Law #12: "Tests lead to Testimony"

Take time to reflect on the list of Respect The Code Laws and use these codes to assist you with Codeswitching & Career Strategies for your Success!

Resources for Personal Development & Career Transitioning

Get certified! Some companies offer it free but if you are unemployed or your current employer doesn't offer it, then go find a webinar that conducts it for cheap or free.

Here's one for Free! The EEOC certification: https://www.compliancetrainingonline.com/eeoc_certification_training.cfm

You may be thinking, "I can't believe there are free certificates and if they are the institute is probably flaky and unheard of!"

Not true! Take a look at some of the list of free online courses to gain certification for a variety of industries.

Free Online College with Accredited Degrees:
*Christian Leadership Institute
http://Christianleadersinstitute.org

*This is the only accredited online college that I can recommend from experience. To attain certifications are free but to earn a bachelor's degree is a generosity driven model

Free Online Courses with certificates:
HarvardX - https://www.edx.org/school/harvardx

Yale Online
http://online.yale.edu/about

Alison
https://alison.com/

Open2Study
https://www.open2study.com/

Coursera

https://www.coursera.org/

Udacity
https://www.udacity.com/

Future
https://www.futurelearn.com/

NPTEL
https://onlinecourses.nptel.ac.in/explorer

OpenLearn
http://www.open.edu/openlearn/

Saylor
http://www.saylor.org/

LINKEDIN TIPS

Linkedin is a social media site designed for professional networking. Most hiring managers and recruiters have Linkedin profiles and you should too. LinkedIn profiles should capture the attention of the person reading it and should help readers understand exactly who you are professionally through your profile.

Here are some tips:
- Don't sound judgmental, cocky, or bias. This is not a time to declare your religious beliefs, your racial preferences, corporations or managers that hurt you, or your prejudices against others. Leave all the personal baggage at home or Facebook if you think you have to do it. Honestly, you shouldn't post those types of opinions on any social media platform. PERIOD. It can make or break your interviewing & selection process.

Be PICTURE PERFECT! Ok ok, no one is truly picture perfect. But I do believe in having a PERFECT PICTURE! A picture with dark lighting, no smile, cleavage, partying, drinking, or including others are all No, No's for LinkedIn and any other professional social media platforms. Especially, if you are planning to get a new career, desire to be taken seriously in your present career, or seeking a promotion. Remove the pics wearing dark shades or really close up shots. Your profile picture should have a plain or bright background. You should be showing some teeth, smile! You should be looking directly at the viewer. Dress for success, wear the outfit that your career typically would wear! At the end of the day social selling works! Social selling is about establishing credibility and giving prospective recruiters or managers a reason to trust you. That starts with your profile photo.

- Headlining! Your headline can be as creative or to the point as you like for it to be."Rock Star Recruiter with strong ability to find unicorns & purple squirrels!" You can be creative in crafting your LinkedIn profile, it doesn't have to be boring!

After completing your LinkedIn page in its entirety, you should have an All Star profile. LinkedIn breaks down your profile strength into 5 different levels.
- Beginner
- Intermediate
- Advanced
- Expert
- All-Star

All Star is the highest level you can attain! But the secret is, it's the profile that normally gets promoted a lot by LinkedIn. Let's try to get you to All Star level!

If you followed the previous instructions plus making sure you have
- 50 or more LinkedIn connections
- Your location added to your profile
- At least two positions listed (If you have never worked in a "real" position add internships, volunteering, or self employment services)
- Your skills (include technical & transferable skills)
- Last but not least SOME form of education. You could even do Hard Knock Life University! Just put your education that you have received whether it be from GED, Community college, High School or traditional college.

Ultimately, LinkedIn is mandatory if you desire to be seen in a professional network.
There are 433 million registered LinkedIn professionals. A whopping 40% of that number actually visits the site every day! We have to understand the power of having our profiles visible for hiring managers, recruiters, speaking engagements, business opportunities etc.

If even half of 433 million viewers were hiring managers taking a look at your profile, what do you think they would say about you?

MOCK INTERVIEW

A Mock interview is a practice round where you give your ALL in order to have a positive and optimal outcome in your interview.
I suggest a mock interview for every position. Here's a couple of tips that I give to my career coaching clients.

First, find out where you will be interviewing. Once you find out the interviewing company, let's break down each step:
1.) Research the company and the department where you will be potentially working. Go to linkedin and find out who you will be interviewing with and research who he/she is connected to and in his department. Look up their Glass Door reviews.

2.) Research the competition. Find out what the company's biggest competitors are doing. Do they have a bigger social media following? What are their reviews on Glass Doors?

3.) Make notes of the best pros and then make a list of the cons on Glass doors.

4.) Print the Job description and highlight the requirements.

5.) Research the interview questions on glass door if any, and write them down.

6.) Use the job description requirements to help create 2 stories that highlight a time where you had to use those particular skill sets.

7.) Describe your ideal working environment. Grab the notes from glass doors that speak positively about the company and use them to help describe only YOUR TRUTH of what the company possesses in comparison to your ideal working environment.

8.) Any Questions? Make sure you ask what happened to the previous person in the position!
    a.) Did they get promoted or did they leave? If they left, what are the biggest take aways you received from your experience with this person and what would you have liked to see him/her do more of while they were in this role?
    b.) On a scale from 1-10, 1 being the worst and 10 being the absolute best, how would you rate the department you currently work in within the company? If a 10, why? If an 8, what could make it into a 10?
    c.) What's the biggest risk you ever took in your current role? If none, in your previous role with the company.
    d.) WHat's a regular day look like for this role?

9.) After they have answered, use their answers to create responses on why you are perfect for the job!

10.) Lastly, Leave on a High Note! Don't give an answer too fast. Do not initiate conversation about money. Always take at least 24 hours before accepting or declining an offer.

Mo Davis is not only an author, she also manages Fresh Talent Sources, a minority owned business.

Fresh Talent Sources is dedicated to coaching businesses, professionals, and ministries into their success.

Monique is also committed to helping unemployed & returning citizens into professional thriving careers through ministry. She tours the nation empowering individuals through training seminars focused on Career Readiness and How to Respect The Code in various environments.

Booking a speaker or trainer for your next college, retention center, nonprofit or corporate function? Reach out to us monique@ftsources.com or 866-702-1205
www.FTSources.com

Index

Acquired page 26

Beast pages 26, 29, 53, 80

Career Assessment pages 16, 20, 80

College pages 14, 18, 21, 26, 31, 85, 88, 91

Counseling pages 20, 72

Coworker pages 25, 62, 63, 66, 67, 71, 74, 76

Development 29, 32, 51, 61, 70, 71

Discern pages 19, 58, 69, 74

Ethics pages 26, 36, 62, 74

Feedback 27, 28, 75

Friend pages 10, 11, 17, 18, 24, 25, 31, 32, 33, 36, 42, 66, 67, 74, 77, 86

Hair pages 16, 20, 21, 34, 39

Identity pages 12, 14, 81

Perfectionist pages 26

Phone pages 24, 43, 55, 62

Poverty pages 21, 31, 85

Praise pages 26, 27, 36, 49

Prideful page 29

Promotion pages 10, 14, 25, 49, 51, 72, 90

Purpose pages 10, 22, 34, 81, 86

Quit pages 27

Rejection pages 20

Self identity pages 12, 14

Script pages 24

Sourcers 26

Stress pages 26

Stubborn page 29

Success pages 10, 11, 12, 13, 14, 17, 18, 19, 20, 31, 32, 38, 42, 49, 54, 66, 76, 85, 86, 87, 90, 95

Virtual pages 26, 51, 80

Voice pages 22, 24, 25

Work behavior pages 26, 75

Respect the Code Dictionary

Beast- A person that is extremely good at something

Big head- A person who allows compliments to get to their mindset or head.

Bosses- Underground Leaders that typically have their own society, business and customs that don't adhere to the laws of the state

Bostonian- A person born and/or raised in Boston, MA

Bubbie - Jewish term of endearment for Grandmother

Career Assessment- Assesses your skills, personality, values, and interests to identify the most optimal career or job placement

Country slang- A slower dialect with shortened words like "fo" instead of "for"

Code switching - Customizing your style speech, body language, and/or actions dependent upon the environment or group of people being addressed

Discern/Discernment- To intuitively perceive from God

Dope boy - A young man who participates in the sell of illegal substances

Hood- The neighborhood where you grew up

Jack of all trades- A person who is sufficient at a lot of things

Lost in the Sauce - The sauce is the everyday chaos, repetition and confusion that goes on in a job, and the individual gets lost in it

Office Norm - Unseen work place understanding and common sense used in the office

Play dumb in order to get smart- Pretending to NOT be savvy or intelligent in specific areas in order to get away with receiving more information

Sourcer- Supports the Recruiting process by generating qualified individuals that match current and future requisitions

Requisitions- Open job orders normally added in the hiring company's applicant tracking system

Wifey- Long term girlfriend but not a wife with a contractual agreement or marriage

References

Stevenson, A. (2010). *Oxford Dictionary of English*. UK: Oxford University Press

Hobson, A. (2004). *Oxford Dictionary of Difficult Words*. UK: Oxford University Press